THE ESSE
MELVILLE

SELECTED BY
ROBERT PENN WARREN

The Essential Poets

Volume 1   The Essential Keats

Volume 2   The Essential Whitman

Volume 3   The Essential Melville

Volume 4   The Essential Blake

FUTURE VOLUMES
WILL INCLUDE

The Essential Wordsworth

The Essential Hopkins

The Essential Hardy

The Essential Clare

The Essential Donne

The Essential Wyatt

The Essential Tennyson

The Essential Browning

The Essential Milton

The Essential Marvell

The Essential Melville

Herman Melville

BORN   1 AUGUST 1819
DIED   28 SEPTEMBER 1891

The Essential
MELVILLE

Selected and with an
Introduction by

ROBERT PENN WARREN

The Ecco Press
New York

Introduction and selection copyright © 1987 by Robert Penn Warren
All rights reserved
Published by The Ecco Press in 1987
18 West 30th Street, New York, N.Y. 10001
Published simultaneously in Canada by Penguin Books Canada Ltd., Ontario
Printed in the United States of America
Designed by Reg Perry

Library of Congress Cataloging in Publication Data
Melville, Herman, 1819–1891.
The essential Melville.

(The Essential poets ; v. 3)
I. Warren, Robert Penn, 1905–   . II. Title.
III. Series: Essential poets (New York, N.Y.) ; v. 3.
PS2382.W3 1987   813'.3   86-24068
ISBN 0-88001-140-8
ISBN 0-88001-141-6 (pbk.)

Painting of Melville by Joseph Oriel Eaton.
Reproduced by permission of Houghton Library,
Harvard University.

Contents

❖❖

INTRODUCTION BY ROBERT PENN WARREN   3

POEMS   15

FROM *BATTLE-PIECES*   15
The Portent   15
Misgivings   15
The Conflict of Convictions   16
The March into Virginia   19
Ball's Bluff   20
A Utilitarian View of the Monitor's Fight   21
Shiloh   22
The House-top   23
On the Photograph of a Corps Commander   24
The College Colonel   25
"The Coming Storm"   26
"Formerly a Slave"   27
On the Slain Collegians   28
Inscription   30
An Uninscribed Monument   30
A Requiem   31
On a Natural Monument   32
Commemorative of a Naval Victory   32
Supplement to *Battle-Pieces*   33

FROM *CLAREL*   *42*
Epilogue   *42*

FROM *JOHN MARR AND OTHER STORIES*   *43*
John Marr (with prose introduction)   *43*
Tom Deadlight (with prose introduction)   *50*
Jack Roy   *51*
The Man-of-War Hawk   *52*
Old Counsel   *53*
The Tuft of Kelp   *53*
The Maldive Shark   *53*
The Berg   *54*
from *Pebbles*   *55*

FROM *TIMOLEON*   *56*
The Ravaged Villa   *56*
Monody   *56*
In a Church of Padua   *56*
from *The Parthenon*   *57*

FROM *UNCOLLECTED POEMS*   58
   Immolated   58
   Pontoosuce   58
   Jonah's Song   61
   Billy in the Darbies   62

ABOUT THE EDITOR   64

The Essential Melville

Introduction

❖❖

By the age of thirty-one, Herman Melville, after a childhood of
wealth, had found himself in a number of various situations: a
common seaman in the forecastle of a ship bound for England, an ad-
venturer among whalers, a survivor on an exotic cannibal island in the
Pacific, an enlisted man in the U.S. Navy, and then a famous writer.
But the fame did not last; in 1851, *Moby Dick*, which years later was to
become one of the most celebrated novels of any century, appeared as a
crashing failure. This was the first of many failures that were to mark
the last forty years of this writer's life. In fact, the world's discovery of
Melville as a poet did not even begin until a few anthology pieces ap-
peared in the 1930s, followed in the 1940s by a small selection of his
poems. Now, a little more than a generation later, some critics would
place his name among the most important American poets of the nine-
teenth century, or even today.

Though Melville had dabbled in verse for some years, it was the Civil
War that in 1866 evoked his first serious poetry, a volume called *Battle-
Pieces*. Perhaps the news value of the subject had encouraged Melville to
this undertaking. But the subject itself did have a soul-stirring and para-
doxical quality congenial to Melville. Melville was certainly a Unionist
and was strongly opposed to slavery, but he was not unaware of the
costs that are sometimes paid even for good ends. For instance, Melville
could foresee what, some fifteen years later, was to disturb another
famous Unionist, Walt Whitman, who would fear that in the new
order created by victory there would be "vast crops of poor, desperate,
dissatisfied, miserably-waged population," which would bring "our
republican experiment" to "an unhealthy failure."

But long before Whitman's forebodings, Melville, in *Battle-Pieces*, in the poem "The Conflict of Convictions," could reflect on the possibility that the new construction of an iron dome on the Capitol to replace the old wooden one might become a dire symbol for the nation's future history:

> *Power unanointed may come —*
> *Dominion (unsought by the free)*
>   *And the Iron Dome,*
> *Stronger for stress and strain,*
> *Fling her huge shadow athwart the main;*
> *But the Founders' dream shall flee.*

Melville saw the possibility of an entrapment in victory however nobly sought. War might be fought for human freedom, but victory might carry its own irony: the possibility of the great modern power state of unbridled capitalism and military ambition might herald a new and disastrous destiny.

A few lines earlier in the poem, Melville had just written:

> *I know a wind of purpose strong —*
>   *It spins against the way it drives.*

What, in other words, are the real forces of history? Even with the most beneficent intentions, can man really determine the meaning of historical events? Or are men only tools determined by a blind mechanism of history?

With this idea we may plunge toward the center of *Battle-Pieces*. Let us turn to the poem "The March into Virginia." Here is the happy march, totally self-confident, toward the First Battle of Manassas, or Bull Run. "All wars are boyish, and are fought by boys," the poet remarked on the childish gaiety of the troops. "Youth must its ignorant impulse lend" to make war possible, but in this instance the Union army was literally accompanied by ladies and gentlemen in carriages, who came to see the sport.

> The banners play, the bugles call,   16
> The air is blue and prodigal.   17
>   No berrying party, pleasure-wooed,   18
> No picnic party in the May,   19
> Ever went less loth than they   20
>   Into that leafy neighborhood.   21

We notice here the implications of the phrase "leafy neighborhood" — a pleasant picnic spot. But there is suddenly the next stanza: those who had fared forth in lightsome files shall

> Perish, enlightened by the vollied glare;   34
> Or shame survive, and, like to adamant,   35
>   The throe of Second Manassas share.   36

Boyhood is over. The boy is "enlightened," instructed.

We have been giving a few quotations and a short paraphrase of "The March into Virginia." But in any real poem this sort of treatment is inadequate for an understanding of its quality, good or bad — even though a reader may *somehow* feel something of the quality of the work. The purpose, in the end, of such a discussion should be to sharpen and clarify a reader's natural awarenesses of what the full and significant impact of a poem may be.

Let us look at the matter of rhythm in the following line:

> Shall die experienced ere three days are spent —   33

Isolated thus, this line seems to be a rather simple five-accent, or pentameter, line. But in full context we may not have such a simple reaction. Just now in the poem we have come from a long section of tetrameter (or four-beat) lines which, in this poem, have a brisk and very clearly marked effect. Now in this sudden and unexpected shift to pentameter the accustomed expectation of the four-beat line remains. Here, however, another factor enters. Here we also naturally know that the initial phrase of line 33 ("Shall die") completes the statement begun back in line 31, for the subject of the verb has been the word *some* ("But some"). So we sense a fulfillment of meaning and a pause after "Shall die." And such a feeling of pause, even though there is no actual pause indicated by punctuation, means that the rest of the line (". . . experienced ere three days are spent") is for a moment felt as a separate tetrameter line with a definite pause, the dash, after it. The word *die* has come with such a finalizing emphasis that the passage might even have been set as follows:

> *Shall die,*
> *Experienced ere three days are spent*

But the point Melville is to make is not mere death to come, but death now in the sudden knowledge of the "vollied glare."

All of the rhythmic effects here are a subtle way of implying the drama of the actual situation.

It may also be remarked that the line now discussed as tetrameter ("Experienced ere three . . .") has a very different rhythm from the usual brisk and almost lilting effect of the long tetrameter passage from lines 12 to 32, in which often the expected iambic foot ($-\acute{\ }$) is changed to a trochee ($\acute{\ }-$) or sometimes merely one accented syllable alone. As an example of the last metrical situation mentioned, we have line 30:

> *Chátting léft and laughing ríght.*

We had been discussing line 33, but this, of course, does not end the sentence. It is punctuated at the end by a dash to indicate that what is to come may be regarded as a development:

> Perish, enlightened by the vollied glare;   34
> Or shame survive, and, like to adamant,   35
> The throe of Second Manassas share.   36

We notice that line 34 is essential to the meaning of the word *experienced* in the preceding line. It defines the meaning of that word. The experience is in facing the fact of what the "vollied glare" means. The boyish troops face the sudden knowledge of what really is. It may be death or it may be what is to follow in lines 35 and 36. The survivors now know what battle is and have had to make some sort of adaptation to that fact.

However, more is involved in this whole passage. Line 33 must find the subject of the word *Perish* and that subject is, as for line 33, the word *some* in line 31.

> But some who this blithe mood present,   31

Thus, the whole passage before this point is bound, one might say, into a unity. But here, with line 34, we have not ended the sentence, for that line ends with a semicolon. Now, line 35 again refers to the "some" who survived the "vollied glare," and overcoming their shame and becoming hardened to danger are able to face the throe (painful convulsion or struggle) of battle which they share with all others, and which may lead to death, perhaps on the same old ground in the Second Manassas. We may notice, too, that the verb *survive* again finds its subject in the word *some* of line 31 and thus binds again all elements of the passage in a single complicated effect.*

---

*We may return to the phrase "vollied glare" and the word *enlightened*. Part of the effect of the passage lies in the fact that the word *enlightened* is a pun. It compresses two meanings. The first, by a kind of metaphor (the first meaning we seize on), is to be "in-

We may notice one more technical feature. In the last line (36) the meter is actually tetrameter, but the "feeling" of the line is much longer. This happens because the line cannot be actually uttered without what may be called a "forced pause." For instance, the transition between *throe* and *of* and that of the demand of the last *s* of *Manassas* and the first of *share* as actually spoken is difficult and forces a pause.

We must never forget that poetry is, in a fundamental way, an *art of sound.* It is not a multiplication table or a telephone book to give information. After some experience, a silent reader has a kind of diminished muscular response, but a real response, as though reading aloud. Often this sense develops unconsciously.

We now turn to the poem "Shiloh," which has a natural relation to our previous poem. But the relation of the poem on the First Battle of Manassas and that at Shiloh Church, near which the Battle of Shiloh occurred, is not one of repetition. "The March" is a movement toward strength against the natural fear that develops at the "vollied glare" and its enlightenment. It is a movement toward deadly action to come, but "Shiloh" is defined as a "Requiem," the result of action.

In "Shiloh" there are no survivors present. Those here are those who were "Foemen at morn" but are "friends at eve." For what, "like a bullet can undeceive"? Action is now followed by a "natural" hush. And with the word *undeceive* the theme of "The March into Virginia" is subtly repeated.

This poem says that enemies are paradoxically friends in the natural end of death which they share. The lesson of the "vollied glare" is that men

structed." The second meaning, which comes in dramatic suddenness, is the actual flash of musketry aimed at those who are to be instructed. Such punning may occasionally be a powerful device for concentration of meaning in poetry.

must learn to endure their "unnatural" fate. Or by implication, to seek new values.

We must not, however, assume that the schooled heroism taught by the "vollied glare" does not have its own laws and values. In fact, much of Melville's poetry involves a paradox. Let us now look at "On the Photograph of a Corps Commander." A lesson not in "Shiloh" is learned in this record. The "Photograph" of the title is that of a federal general, a hero of the Battle of Spotsylvania Courthouse. However, the meaning of the poem goes beyond that fact to a generalization:

> Nothing can lift the heart of man
> Like manhood in a fellow-man.

Heroism and manhood: each has its own lessons to teach. But what is there to be learned by the man, the hero, who survives his own heroism? "The College Colonel" is one of Melville's most explicit poems on this subject. Here Melville had, again, a real model for its colonel, the figure of the gallant, wounded young man who, after all heroism and personal suffering on the battlefield and in prison, later leads his old command in a celebratory parade. But in the poem the celebration brings to the hero "alloy"—foreign matter to be mixed with any feeling of triumph. As the poem puts it, there now comes "what *truth* to him."

Melville does not answer his own question. But at least there is no self-congratulation, no proud preening. The same issue arises in other poems, most obviously in "Inscription for Marye's Heights," which is the celebration of an episode in the Battle of Fredericksburg. There, in the face of obvious disaster, the federal attackers bravely follow an idiotic command, and their soldierly death is more deserving of a monument than any victory could be.

But set against the valor of those who gallantly go to sure defeat, we may cite "Commemorative of a Naval Victory." Here the hero lives on to see his own personal fame:

> *Repose is yours—your deed is known*
> *It musks the amber wine*

But now Melville, in the same tone used to address "The College Colonel," asks what fame is:

> *There's a light and a shadow on every man*
> *Who at last attains his lifted mark—*
> *Nursing through night the ethereal spark.*
> *Elate he can never be;*
> *He feels that spirits which glad had hailed his worth.*
> *Sleep in oblivion. —The shark*
> *Glides white through the phosphorus sea.*

This poem, one of Melville's meditations on fame (on the fame which, after *Moby Dick*, he himself would never know again), shows in the beginning of that last stanza an image that summarizes the condition of the naval hero:

> *But seldom the laurel wreath is seen*
> *Unmixed with pensive pansies dark*

That is, the presence of the laurel implies that the accompanying pansies in their pensiveness suggest sadness and give an ambiguity to the hero's fame. Those in the battle who did not achieve fame but had shown courage would have generously applauded the hero's fame even if now they

> *Sleep in oblivion. —The shark*
> *Glides white through the phosphorus sea.*

The applauded hero may ask why it is he who survives among the thousands of valiant men who have died but, if living, would have generously praised his own worth. And here we must notice the brilliant moment at the end of the poem: here against the background of a cele-

bratory banquet the actual scene of the naval battle is seemingly rein-
acted, with the dead bodies of the unsung heroes floating down amidst
the debris of battle as the shark's white belly turns so that the under-
slung jaws seize a victim, a hero who will go unsung. This shark sud-
denly, shockingly, obscures the whole banquet scene by an image: the
reality behind heroism.

It is only natural that his years of constant failure should have haunted
Melville in his poetry. In his brief prose introduction to *Clarel*, his ob-
session with failure is quite specific. There Melville states that he awaits
with indifference the fate of the new work. The themes of hardiness and
courage in the face of even certain failure appear again and again. In the
brief poem "Old Counsel" the exhortation is to the "Young Master of a
California Clipper" to be not "over-elate," for the cry

> All hands save ship! *has startled dreamers.*

In "The Tuft of Kelp," the kelp is not only "purer" because of the
depth of the lonely sea, but bitterer too. In another poem, "The Maldive
Shark," the sleepy little pilot fish that accompany the shark find asylum
"in jaws of the Fates" and we remember that in another poem "storms
are formed behind the storms we feel." This notion echoes the idea in
"The Conflict of Convictions" of the winds of History. Behind the
storm of the Civil War which Melville experienced, another had been
brewing, at least what Melville, or Walt Whitman, would have con-
sidered a storm.

After the victory, the completion of a new iron dome of the Capitol,
and the publication of *Battle-Pieces*, William Vanderbilt (son of the old
"Commodore") rose to explain to a congressional committee that no-
body could now stop the "new men" who now ran the country.

Naturally, Melville, who had long since written of that "Iron Dome"
and who had dreamed a kind of peace far different from what had actu-

ally happened, was not the man invited to write the "cantata" to be presented at the great Centennial celebration of the founding of the United States. The cantata was done by Sidney Lanier, a safe choice who ruffled no feathers; his work was vapid, harmless, and unmemorable.

Melville, however, had written his own poem published in the year of the Centennial celebration, 1876: *Clarel.*

As we look back over more than a century, *Clarel*, in its basic meaning, seems vastly better than Lanier's work for the occasion of the cantata. The chief character, Clarel, is a theological student who has lost his faith and now returns to the Holy Land in hope of renewing that faith. But there he finds a philosophical hodgepodge of modernity, even among the people who have come to visit the Holy Land, a hodgepodge including modern, watered-down Christianity, revolutionaries of the then modern type, an ex-Confederate officer turned cynical adventurer, a modern scientist to whom science is the only truth, a Yankee religious fanatic turned Jew, a fallen-away Catholic, and a beautiful girl who brings human love to Clarel. But in the violence of the Holy Land she is killed, and he, Clarel, is left alone in modernity and its inscrutability.

Unlike Sidney Lanier, who had offered a patchwork to smooth over any questions concerning the Civil War, Melville offered, in the same year, a vision of the problems facing civilization. But *Clarel* is not a successful poem. It is inordinately long, with many hasty and dull sections which, however effective thematically, have not been realized poetically. Nevertheless, for all its faults and poetic failures, it does offer certain impressive patches, some of which are even poetically impressive. Many others are impressive philosophically, thematically, or dramatically. Rarely given the attention it deserves, *Clarel* at least remains a fundamentally necessary document of our cultural history.

After the failure of *Clarel*, which a rich relative of Melville's wife had financed, Melville remained a poet, but never again offered any work to a publisher. He continued to write but fell from any public view. Each of the two thin volumes of poems of later years were printed in an edition of only a few copies designed primarily as gifts for friends. His wife, who had come into an inheritance, supported him in his last years, for he was no longer working at his meager job at the Customs, and gave him an allowance for buying books and such things, and even for the printing of his poems.

So poems of this last period may be found in the little volumes, *John Marr and Other Sailors* (1888) and *Timoleon* (1891)—the latter being published a few months before the author's death. But in the last years, Melville had been deeply absorbed in another work of fiction and a related poem—the short novel *Billy Budd* and the accompanying poem, "Billy in the Darbies."

These two works are certainly among Melville's several masterpieces. They seem to have had a slow growth from a painful aspect of Melville's personal life apart from his chronic failures in writing, from *Moby Dick* forward. Both *Billy Budd* and its accompanying poem seem to have started out as merely a prose headnote (such as those that appear in *John Marr and Other Sailors*). But somewhere along the way this idea became crucially different, modified by two events in Melville's own life, one many years before the other. The early crucial event was the suicide of Melville's first son, Malcolm, who had quarreled with his father. Now, thirty years later, the second son, Stanwix, a confused failure all his life, was reported dead. The miserable story of Stanwix seems to have stirred the father's old feelings about the suicide of Malcolm, and the original idea of a poem about a tough old sailor, with a prose headnote, presumably developed into what we now have in *Billy Budd*, a father-son story.

In the novel, the father, Captain Vere, commander of a British man-of-war, condemns Billy for a murder even though Vere knows that Billy, though he had actually struck dead an evil tormentor, is psychologically innocent. After all, Billy is nothing but a charming "barbarian," beloved and admired by the whole crew. But Vere, as a naval officer, must condemn him to be hanged at the yardarm the next morning. Furthermore, this is a sort of version of the biblical story of Abraham and Isaac. Vere, who has somehow realized that the boy is his own bastard son, must nevertheless act out his duty as a commander.

The recognition scene of father and son is not given in the novel, but it is clear that Billy, in his "barbarian" generosity, knows and accepts Vere as his father, as well as his judge. The actual scene of the hanging becomes a kind of mystical moment, and all the crew feel that impact. Crewmen actually take chips of the spar from which Billy had been hanged, and regard such relics as though "a piece of the Cross."

This compressed summary, which gives no sense of the power of the novel, is necessary to grasp the meaning of the poem "Billy in the Darbies."

In the novel the body of Billy is drawn up by the rope against "a vapory fleece hanging low in the East shot through with some soft glory as of the fleece of the lamb of God." Against that moment, the moment as presumably experienced by the hardened crew, we come to "Billy in the Darbies"—the literal human being who, even as a sufferer, recognizes the truly tragic situation and now feels the metal of the cuff irons merely as a minor inconvenience. But at the end of the poem Billy has not yet left the deck and the sentry. He is merely dreaming into his death. He can address the actual sentry, as he lies there, already feeling the oozy weeds not the "darbies." But notice the last word "twist." It is not a sleepy or restful word. It hints at the violence which in the poem is already overpassed, but in fact is to come.

Billy Budd was not published until 1924, thirty-three years after Melville's death. This lapse of time between the composition and the publication of the two works, novel and poem, somehow seems to fit the pattern of Melville's life. It also fits the pattern of his life that both the novel and the poem should now be regarded as masterly.

—ROBERT PENN WARREN

Poems

❖❖

FROM *BATTLE-PIECES*

The Portent

Hanging from the beam,
   Slowly swaying (such the law),
Gaunt the shadow on your green,
   Shenandoah!
The cut is on the crown
(Lo, John Brown),
And the stabs shall heal no more.

Hidden in the cap
   Is the anguish none can draw;
So your future veils its face,
   Shenandoah!
But the streaming beard is shown
(Weird John Brown),
The meteor of the war.

Misgivings

When ocean-clouds over inland hills
   Sweep storming in late autumn brown,
And horror the sodden valley fills,

And the spire falls crashing in the town,
I muse upon my country's ills—
The tempest bursting from the waste of Time
On the world's fairest hope linked with man's foulest crime.

Nature's dark side is heeded now—
   (Ah! optimist-cheer disheartened flown)—
A child may read the moody brow
   Of yon black mountain lone.
With shouts the torrents down the gorges go,
And storms are formed behind the storm we feel:
The hemlock shakes in the rafter, the oak in the driving keel.

The Conflict of Convictions

On starry heights
   A bugle wails the long recall;
Derision stirs the deep abyss,
   Heaven's ominous silence over all.
Return, return, O eager Hope,
   And face man's latter fall.
Events, they make the dreamers quail;
Satan's old age is strong and hale,
A disciplined captain, gray in skill,
And Raphael a white enthusiast still;
Dashed aims, at which Christ's martyrs pale,
Shall Mammon's slaves fulfill?

   (Dismantle the fort,
   Cut down the fleet—
   Battle no more shall be!
   While the fields for fight in æons to come
   Congeal beneath the sea.)

The terrors of truth and dart of death
    To faith alike are vain;
Though comets, gone a thousand years,
    Return again,
Patient she stands—she can no more—
And waits, nor heeds she waxes hoar.

(At a stony gate,
A statue of stone,
Weed overgrown—
Long 'twill wait!)

But God his former mind retains,
    Confirms his old decree;
The generations are inured to pains,
    And strong Necessity
Surges, and heaps Time's strand with wrecks.
    The People spread like a weedy grass,
    The thing they will they bring to pass,
And prosper to the apoplex.
The rout it herds around the heart,
    The ghost is yielded in the gloom;
Kings wag their heads—Now save thyself
    Who wouldst rebuild the world in bloom.

(Tide-mark
And top of the ages' strife,
Verge where they called the world to come,
The last advance of life—
Ha ha, the rust on the Iron Dome!)

Nay, but revere the hid event;
    In the cloud a sword is girded on,
I mark a twinkling in the tent

Of Michael the warrior one.
Senior wisdom suits not now,
The light is on the youthful brow.

> (*Ay, in caves the miner see:*
> *His forehead bears a blinking light;*
> *Darkness so he feebly braves—*
> *A meagre wight!*)

But He who rules is old—is old;
Ah! faith is warm, but heaven with age is cold.

> (*Ho ho, ho ho,*
> *The cloistered doubt*
> *Of olden times*
> *Is blurted out!*)

The Ancient of Days forever is young,
  Forever the scheme of Nature thrives;
I know a wind in purpose strong—
  It spins *against* the way it drives.
What if the gulfs their slimed foundations bare?
So deep must the stones be hurled
Whereon the throes of ages rear
The final empire and the happier world.

> (*The poor old Past,*
> *The Future's slave,*
> *She drudged through pain and crime*
> *To bring about the blissful Prime,*
> *Then—perished. There's a grave!*)

Power unanointed may come—
Dominion (unsought by the free)

And the Iron Dome,
Stronger for stress and strain,
Fling her huge shadow athwart the main;
But the Founders' dream shall flee.
Age after age shall be
As age after age has been,
(From man's changeless heart their way they win);
And death be busy with all who strive—
Death, with silent negative.

YEA AND NAY—
EACH HATH HIS SAY;
BUT GOD HE KEEPS THE MIDDLE WAY.
NONE WAS BY
WHEN HE SPREAD THE SKY;
WISDOM IS VAIN, AND PROPHESY.

The March into Virginia

ENDING IN THE FIRST MANASSAS

Did all the lets and bars appear
    To every just or larger end,
Whence should come the trust and cheer?
    Youth must its ignorant impulse lend—
Age finds place in the rear.
    All wars are boyish, and are fought by boys,
The champions and enthusiasts of the state:
    Turbid ardors and vain joys
        Not barrenly abate—
    Stimulants to the power mature,
        Preparatives of fate.

Who here forecasteth the event?
What heart but spurns at precedent
And warnings of the wise,
Contemned foreclosures of surprise?
The banners play, the bugles call,
The air is blue and prodigal.
   No berrying party, pleasure-wooed,
No picnic party in the May,
Ever went less loth than they
   Into that leafy neighborhood.
In Bacchic glee they file toward Fate,
Moloch's uninitiate;
Expectancy, and glad surmise
Of battle's unknown mysteries.
All they feel is this: 'tis glory,
A rapture sharp, though transitory,
Yet lasting in belaureled story.
So they gayly go to fight,
Chatting left and laughing right.

But some who this blithe mood present,
   As on in lightsome files they fare,
Shall die experienced ere three days are spent—
   Perish, enlightened by the vollied glare;
Or shame survive, and, like to adamant,
   The throe of Second Manassas share.

Ball's Bluff

A REVERIE

One noonday, at my window in the town,
   I saw a sight—saddest that eyes can see—

Young soldiers marching lustily
        Unto the wars,
With fifes, and flags in mottoed pageantry;
    While all the porches, walks, and doors
Were rich with ladies cheering royally.

They moved like Juny morning on the wave,
    Their hearts were fresh as clover in its prime
    (It was the breezy summer time),
        Life throbbed so strong,
How should they dream that Death in a rosy clime
        Would come to thin their shining throng?
Youth feels immortal, like the gods sublime.

Weeks passed; and at my window, leaving bed,
    By night I mused, of easeful sleep bereft,
    On those brave boys (Ah War! thy theft);
        Some marching feet
Found pause at last by cliffs Potomac cleft;
        Wakeful I mused, while in the street
Far footfalls died away till none were left.

A Utilitarian View of the Monitor's Fight

Plain be the phrase, yet apt the verse,
    More ponderous than nimble;
For since grimed War here laid aside
His Orient pomp, 'twould ill befit
        Overmuch to ply
    The rhyme's barbaric cymbal.

Hail to victory without the gaud
    Of glory; zeal that needs no fans

Of banners; plain mechanic power
Plied cogently in War now placed—
     Where War belongs—
     Among the trades and artisans.

Yet this was battle, and intense—
     Beyond the strife of fleets heroic;
Deadlier, closer, calm 'mid storm;
No passion; all went on by crank,
          Pivot, and screw,
     And calculations of caloric.

Needless to dwell; the story's known.
     The ringing of those plates on plates
Still ringeth round the world—
The clangor of that blacksmiths' fray.
          The anvil-din
     Resounds this message from the Fates:

War shall yet be, and to the end;
     But war-paint shows the streaks of weather;
War yet shall be, but warriors
Are now but operatives; War's made
          Less grand than Peace,
     And a singe runs through lace and feather.

Shiloh

A REQUIEM

Skimming lightly, wheeling still,
     The swallows fly low

Over the field in clouded days,
    The forest-field of Shiloh—
Over the field where April rain
Solaced the parched ones stretched in pain
Through the pause of night
That followed the Sunday fight
    Around the church of Shiloh—
The church so lone, the log-built one,
That echoed to many a parting groan
        And natural prayer
    Of dying foemen mingled there—
Foemen at morn, but friends at eve—
    Fame or country least their care:
(What like a bullet can undeceive!)
    But now they lie low,
While over them the swallows skim,
    And all is hushed at Shiloh.

The House-top

A NIGHT PIECE

No sleep. The sultriness pervades the air
And binds the brain—a dense oppression, such
As tawny tigers feel in matted shades,
Vexing their blood and making apt for ravage.
Beneath the stars the roofy desert spreads
Vacant as Libya. All is hushed near by.
Yet fitfully from far breaks a mixed surf
Of muffled sound, the Atheist roar of riot.
Yonder, where parching Sirius set in drought,
Balefully glares red Arson—there—and there.
The Town is taken by its rats—ship-rats

And rats of the wharves. All civil charms
And priestly spells which late held hearts in awe—
Fear-bound, subjected to a better sway
Than sway of self; these like a dream dissolve,
And man rebounds whole æons back in nature.
Hail to the low dull rumble, dull and dead,
And ponderous drag that shakes the wall.
Wise Draco comes, deep in the midnight roll
Of black artillery; he comes, though late;
In code corroborating Calvin's creed
And cynic tyrannies of honest kings;
He comes, nor parlies; and the Town, redeemed,
Gives thanks devout; nor, being thankful, heeds
The grimy slur on the Republic's faith implied,
Which holds that Man is naturally good,
And—more—is Nature's Roman, never to be scourged.

On the Photograph of a Corps Commander

Ay, man is manly. Here you see
    The warrior-carriage of the head,
And brave dilation of the frame;
    And lighting all, the soul that led
In Spottsylvania's charge to victory,
    Which justifies his fame.

A cheering picture. It is good
    To look upon a Chief like this,
In whom the spirit moulds the form.
    Here favoring Nature, oft remiss,
With eagle mien expressive has endued
    A man to kindle strains that warm.

Trace back his lineage, and his sires,
    Yeoman or noble, you shall find
Enrolled with men of Agincourt,
    Heroes who shared great Harry's mind.
Down to us come the knightly Norman fires,
    And front the Templars bore.

Nothing can lift the heart of man
    Like manhood in a fellow-man.
The thought of heaven's great King afar
    But humbles us — too weak to scan;
But manly greatness men can span,
    And feel the bonds that draw.

The College Colonel

He rides at their head;
    A crutch by his saddle just slants in view,
One slung arm is in splints, you see,
    Yet he guides his strong steed — how coldly too.

He brings his regiment home —
    Not as they filed two years before,
But a remnant half-tattered, and battered, and worn,
Like castaway sailors, who — stunned
        By the surf's loud roar,
    Their mates dragged back and seen no more —
Again and again breast the surge,
    And at last crawl, spent, to shore.

A still rigidity and pale —
    An Indian aloofness lones his brow;
He has lived a thousand years

Compressed in battle's pains and prayers,
    Marches and watches slow.

There are welcoming shouts, and flags;
    Old men off hat to the Boy,
Wreaths from gay balconies fall at his feet,
    But to *him*—there comes alloy.

It is not that a leg is lost,
    It is not that an arm is maimed,
It is not that the fever has racked—
    Self he has long disclaimed.

But all through the Seven Days' Fight,
    And deep in the Wilderness grim,
And in the field-hospital tent,
    And Petersburg crater, and dim
Lean brooding in Libby, there came—
    Ah heaven!—what *truth* to him.

"The Coming Storm"

A Picture by S. R. Gifford, and owned by E.B.
Included in the N.A. Exhibition, April, 1865

All feeling hearts must feel for him
    Who felt this picture. Presage dim—
Dim inklings from the shadowy sphere
    Fixed him and fascinated here.

A demon-cloud like the mountain one
    Burst on a spirit as mild

As this urned lake, the home of shades.
   But Shakespeare's pensive child

Never the lines had lightly scanned,
   Steeped in fable, steeped in fate;
The Hamlet in his heart was 'ware,
   Such hearts can antedate.

No utter surprise can come to him
   Who reaches Shakespeare's core;
That which we seek and shun is there—
   Man's final lore.

"Formerly a Slave"

An idealized Portrait, by E. Vedder, in the
Spring Exhibition of the National Academy, 1865

The sufferance of her race is shown,
   And retrospect of life,
Which now too late deliverance dawns upon;
   Yet is she not at strife.

Her children's children they shall know
   The good withheld from her;
And so her reverie takes prophetic cheer—
   In spirit she sees the stir

Far down the depth of thousand years,
   And marks the revel shine;
Her dusky face is lit with sober light,
   Sibylline, yet benign.

On the Slain Collegians

Youth is the time when hearts are large,
    And stirring wars
Appeal to the spirit which appeals in turn
    To the blade it draws.
If woman incite, and duty show
    (Though made the mask of Cain),
Or whether it be Truth's sacred cause,
    Who can aloof remain
That shares youth's ardor, uncooled by the snow
    Of wisdom or sordid gain?

The liberal arts and nurture sweet
Which give his gentleness to man—
    Train him to honor, lend him grace
Through bright examples meet—
That culture which makes never wan
With underminings deep, but holds
    The surface still, its fitting place,
    And so gives sunniness to the face
And bravery to the heart; what troops
    Of generous boys in happiness thus bred—
    Saturnians through life's Tempe led,
Went from the North and came from the South,
With golden mottoes in the mouth,
    To lie down midway on a bloody bed.

Woe for the homes of the North,
And woe for the seats of the South:
All who felt life's spring in prime,
And were swept by the wind of their place and time—
    All lavish hearts, on whichever side,
Of birth urbane or courage high,

Armed them for the stirring wars—
Armed them—some to die.
      Apollo-like in pride,
Each would slay his Python—caught
The maxims in his temple taught—
   Aflame with sympathies whose blaze
Perforce enwrapped him—social laws,
   Friendship and kin, and by-gone days—
Vows, kisses—every heart unmoors,
And launches into the seas of wars.
What could they else—North or South?
Each went forth with blessings given
By priests and mothers in the name of Heaven;
      And honor in both was chief.
Warred one for Right, and one for Wrong?
So be it; but they both were young—
Each grape to his cluster clung,
All their elegies are sung.

The anguish of maternal hearts
   Must search for balm divine;
But well the striplings bore their fated parts
   (The heavens all parts assign)—
Never felt life's care or cloy.
Each bloomed and died an unabated Boy;
Nor dreamed what death was—thought it mere
Sliding into some vernal sphere.
They knew the joy, but leaped the grief,
Like plants that flower ere comes the leaf—
Which storms lay low in kindly doom,
And kill them in their flush of bloom.

Inscription

for Marye's Heights, Fredericksburg

To them who crossed the flood
And climbed the hill, with eyes
  Upon the heavenly flag intent,
  And through the deathful tumult went
Even unto death: to them this Stone—
Erect, where they were overthrown—
  Of more than victory the monument.

An Uninscribed Monument

on One of the Battle-fields of the Wilderness

Silence and Solitude may hint
  (Whose home is in yon piny wood)
What I, though tableted, could never tell—
The din which here befell,
  And striving of the multitude.
The iron cones and spheres of death
  Set round me in their rust,
    These, too, if just,
Shall speak with more than animated breath.
  Thou who beholdest, if thy thought,
Not narrowed down to personal cheer,
Take in the import of the quiet here—
  The after-quiet—the calm full fraught;
Thou too wilt silent stand—
Silent as I, and lonesome as the land.

A Requiem

for Soldiers Lost in Ocean Transports

When, after storms that woodlands rue,
   To valleys comes atoning dawn,
The robins blithe their orchard-sports renew;
   And meadow-larks, no more withdrawn,
Caroling fly in the languid blue;
The while, from many a hid recess,
Alert to partake the blessedness,
The pouring mites their airy dance pursue.
   So, after ocean's ghastly gales,
When laughing light of hoyden morning breaks,
    Every finny hider wakes—
From vaults profound swims up with glittering scales;
   Through the delightsome sea he sails,
With shoals of shining tiny things
Frolic on every wave that flings
   Against the prow its showery spray;
All creatures joying in the morn,
Save them forever from joyance torn,
   Whose bark was lost where now the dolphins play;
Save them that by the fabled shore,
   Down the pale stream are washed away,
Far to the reef of bones are borne;
   And never revisits them the light,
Nor sight of long-sought land and pilot more;
   Nor heed they now the lone bird's flight
Round the lone spar where mid-sea surges pour.

On a Natural Monument

in a Field of Georgia

No trophy this—a Stone unhewn,
   And stands where here the field immures
The nameless brave whose palms are won.
Outcast they sleep; yet fame is nigh—
   Pure fame of deeds, not doers;
Nor deeds of men who bleeding die
   In cheer of hymns that round them float:
In happy dreams such close the eye.
But withering famine slowly wore,
   And slowly fell disease did gloat.
Even Nature's self did aid deny;
They choked in horror the pensive sigh.
   Yea, off from home sad Memory bore
(Though anguished Yearning heaved that way),
Lest wreck of reason might befall.
   As men in gales shun the lee shore,
Though there the homestead be, and call,
And thitherward winds and waters sway—
As such lorn mariners, so fared they.
But naught shall now their peace molest.
   Their fame is this: they did endure—
Endure, when fortitude was vain
To kindle any approving strain
Which they might hear. To these who rest,
   This healing sleep alone was sure.

Commemorative of a Naval Victory

Sailors there are of gentlest breed,
   Yet strong, like every goodly thing;

The discipline of arms refines,
   And the wave gives tempering.
   The damasked blade its beam can fling;
It lends the last grave grace:
The hawk, the hound, and sworded nobleman
   In Titian's picture for a king,
Are of hunter or warrior race.

In social halls a favored guest
   In years that follow victory won,
How sweet to feel your festal fame
   In woman's glance instinctive thrown:
   Repose is yours—your deed is known,
It musks the amber wine;
It lives, and sheds a light from storied days
   Rich as October sunsets brown,
Which make the barren place to shine.

But seldom the laurel wreath is seen
   Unmixed with pensive pansies dark;
There's a light and a shadow on every man
   Who at last attains his lifted mark—
   Nursing through night the ethereal spark.
Elate he never can be;
He feels that spirits which glad had hailed his worth,
   Sleep in oblivion.—The shark
Glides white through the phosphorus sea.

Supplement to *Battle-Pieces*

. . . It is more than a year since the memorable surrender, but events have not yet rounded themselves into completion. Not justly can we complain of this. There has been an upheaval affecting the basis of things; to altered circumstances complicated adaptations are to be made; there are difficulties great and novel. But is Reason still waiting for Passion to spend itself? We have sung of the soldiers and sailors, but who shall hymn the politicians?

In view of the infinite desirableness of Re-establishment, and considering that, so far as feeling is concerned, it depends not mainly on the temper in which the South regards the North, but rather conversely; one who never was a blind adherent feels constrained to submit some thoughts, counting on the indulgence of his countrymen.

And, first, it may be said that, if among the feelings and opinions growing immediately out of a great civil convulsion, there are any which time shall modify or do away, they are presumably those of a less temperate and charitable cast.

There seems no reason why patriotism and narrowness should go together, or why intellectual impartiality should be confounded with political trimming, or why serviceable truth should keep cloistered because not partisan. Yet the work of Reconstruction, if admitted to be feasible at all, demands little but common sense and Christian charity. Little but these? These are much.

Some of us are concerned because as yet the South shows no penitence. But what exactly do we mean by this? Since down to the close of the war she never confessed any for braving it, the only penitence now left her is that which springs solely from the sense of discomfiture; and since this evidently would be a contrition hypocritical, it would be unworthy in us to demand it. Certain it is that penitence, in the sense of voluntary humiliation, will never be displayed. Nor does this afford just ground for unreserved condemnation. It is enough, for all practical purposes, if the South have been taught by the terrors of civil war to feel that Secession, like Slavery, is against Destiny; that both now lie buried in one grave; that her fate is linked with ours; and that together we comprise the Nation.

The clouds of heroes who battled for the Union it is needless to eulogize here. But how of the soldiers on the other side? And when of a free community we name the soldiers, we thereby name the people. It was in subserviency to the slave-interest that Secession was plotted; but it was under the plea, plausibly urged, that certain inestimable rights guaranteed by the Constitution were directly menaced, that the people of the South were cajoled into revolution. Through the arts of the conspirators and the perversity of fortune, the most sensitive love of liberty was entrapped into the support of a war whose implied end was the erecting in our advanced century of an Anglo-American empire based upon the systematic degradation of man.

Spite this clinging reproach, however, signal military virtues and achievements have conferred upon the Confederate arms historic fame, and upon certain of the commanders a renown extending beyond the sea—a renown which we of the North could not suppress, even if we would. In personal character, also, not a few of the military leaders of the South enforce forbearance; the memory of others the North refrains from disparaging; and some, with more or less of reluctance, she can respect. Posterity, sympathizing with our convictions, but removed from our passions, may perhaps go farther here. If George IV. could, out of the graceful instinct of a gentleman, raise an honorable monument in the great fane of Christendom over the remains of the enemy of his dynasty, Charles Edward, the invader of England and victor in the rout at Preston Pans—upon whose head the king's ancestor but one reign removed had set a price—is it probable that the grandchildren of General Grant will pursue with rancor, or slur by sour neglect, the memory of Stonewall Jackson?

But the South herself is not wanting in recent histories and biographies which record the deeds of her chieftains—writings freely published at the North by loyal houses, widely read here, and with a deep though saddened interest. By students of the war such works are hailed as welcome accessories, and tending to the completeness of the record.

Supposing a happy issue out of present perplexities, then, in the generation next to come, Southerners there will be yielding allegiance to the Union, feeling all their interests bound up in it, and yet cherishing unrebuked that kind of feeling for the memory of the soldiers of the fallen Confederacy that Burns, Scott, and the Ettrick Shepherd felt for the memory of the gallant clansmen ruined through their fidelity to the

Stuarts — a feeling whose passion was tempered by the poetry imbuing it, and which in no wise affected their loyalty to the Georges, and which, it may be added, indirectly contributed excellent things to literature. But, setting this view aside, dishonorable would it be in the South were she willing to abandon to shame the memory of brave men who with signal personal disinterestedness warred in her behalf, though from motives, as we believe, so deplorably astray.

Patriotism is not baseness, neither is it inhumanity. The mourners who this summer bear flowers to the mounds of the Virginian and Georgian dead are, in their domestic bereavement and proud affection, as sacred in the eye of Heaven as are those who go with similar offerings of tender grief and love into the cemeteries of our Northern martyrs. And yet, in one aspect, how needless to point the contrast.

Cherishing such sentiments, it will hardly occasion surprise that, in looking over the battle-pieces in the foregoing collection, I have been tempted to withdraw or modify some of them, fearful lest in presenting, though but dramatically and by way of a poetic record, the passions and epithets of civil war, I might be contributing to a bitterness which every sensible American must wish at an end. So, too, with the emotion of victory as reproduced on some pages, and particularly toward the close. It should not be construed into an exultation misapplied — an exultation as ungenerous as unwise, and made to minister, however indirectly, to that kind of censoriousness too apt to be produced in certain natures by success after trying reverses. Zeal is not of necessity religion, neither is it always of the same essence with poetry or patriotism.

There were excesses which marked the conflict, most of which are perhaps inseparable from a civil strife so intense and prolonged, and involving warfare in some border countries new and imperfectly civilized. Barbarities also there were, for which the Southern people collectively can hardly be held responsible, though perpetrated by ruffians in their name. But surely other qualities — exalted ones — courage and fortitude matchless, were likewise displayed, and largely; and justly may these be held the characteristic traits, and not the former.

In this view, what Northern writer, however patriotic, but must revolt from acting on paper a part any way akin to that of the live dog to the dead lion; and yet it is right to rejoice for our triumph, so far as it may justly imply an advance for our whole country and for humanity.

Let it be held no reproach to any one that he pleads for reasonable consideration for our late enemies, now stricken down and unavoidably debarred, for the time, from speaking through authorized agencies for themselves. Nothing has been urged here in the foolish hope of conciliating those men — few in number, we trust — who have resolved never to be reconciled to the Union. On such hearts every thing is thrown away except it be religious commiseration, and the sincerest. Yet let them call to mind that unhappy Secessionist, not a military man, who with impious alacrity fired the first shot of the Civil War at Sumter, and a little more than four years afterward fired the last one into his own heart at Richmond.

Noble was the gesture into which patriotic passion surprised the people in a utilitarian time and country; yet the glory of the war falls short of its pathos — a pathos which now at last ought to disarm all animosity.

How many and earnest thoughts still rise, and how hard to repress them. We feel what past years have been, and years, unretarded years, shall come. May we all have moderation; may we all show candor. Though, perhaps, nothing could ultimately have averted the strife, and though to treat of human actions is to deal wholly with second causes, nevertheless, let us not cover up or try to extenuate what, humanly speaking, is the truth — namely, that those unfraternal denunciations, continued through years, and which at last inflamed to deeds that ended in bloodshed, were reciprocal; and that, had the preponderating strength and the prospect of its unlimited increase lain on the other side, on ours might have lain those actions which now in our late opponents we stigmatize under the name of Rebellion. As frankly let us own — what it would be unbecoming to parade were foreigners concerned — that our triumph was won not more by skill and bravery than by superior resources and crushing numbers; that it was a triumph, too, over a people for years politically misled by designing men, and also by some honestly-erring men, who from their position could not have been otherwise than broadly influential; a people who, though, indeed, they sought to perpetuate the curse of slavery, and even extend it, were not the authors of it, but (less fortunate, not less righteous than we) were the fated inheritors; a people who, having a like origin with ourselves, share essentially in whatever worthy qualities we may possess. No one can add to the lasting reproach which hopeless defeat has now cast upon Secession by withholding the recognition of these verities.

Surely we ought to take it to heart that that kind of pacification, based upon principles operating equally all over the land, which lovers of their country yearn for, and which our arms, though signally triumphant, did not bring about, and which law-making, however anxious, or energetic, or repressive, never by itself can achieve, may yet be largely aided by generosity of sentiment public and private. Some revisionary legislation and adaptive is indispensable; but with this should harmoniously work another kind of prudence, not unallied with entire magnanimity. Benevolence and policy — Christianity and Machiavelli — dissuade from penal severities toward the subdued. Abstinence here is as obligatory as considerate care for our unfortunate fellow-men late in bonds, and, if observed, would equally prove to be wise forecast. The great qualities of the South, those attested in the War, we can perilously alienate, or we may make them nationally available at need.

The blacks, in their infant pupilage to freedom, appeal to the sympathies of every humane mind. The paternal guardianship which for the interval government exercises over them was prompted equally by duty and benevolence. Yet such kindliness should not be allowed to exclude kindliness to communities who stand nearer to us in nature. For the future of the freed slaves we may well be concerned; but the future of the whole country, involving the future of the blacks, urges a paramount claim upon our anxiety. Effective benignity, like the Nile, is not narrow in its bounty, and true policy is always broad. To be sure, it is vain to seek to glide, with moulded words, over the difficulties of the situation. And for them who are neither partisans, nor enthusiasts, nor theorists, nor cynics, there are some doubts not readily to be solved. And there are fears. Why is not the cessation of war now at length attended with the settled calm of peace? Wherefore in a clear sky do we still turn our eyes toward the South, as the Neapolitan, months after the eruption, turns his toward Vesuvius? Do we dread lest the repose may be deceptive? In the recent convulsion has the crater but shifted? Let us revere that sacred uncertainty which forever impends over men and nations. Those of us who always abhorred slavery as an atheistical iniquity, gladly we join in the exulting chorus of humanity over its downfall. But we should remember that emancipation was accomplished not by deliberate legislation; only through agonized violence could so mighty a result be effected. In our natural solicitude to confirm the benefit of liberty to the blacks, let us forbear from measures of dubious constitutional rightfulness toward our white countrymen—measures of a nature to provoke, among other of the last evils, exterminating hatred of race toward race. In imagination let us place ourselves in the unprecedented position of the Southerners—their position as regards the millions of ignorant manumitted slaves in their midst, for whom some of us now claim the suffrage. Let us be Christians toward our fellow-whites, as well as philanthropists toward the blacks, our fellow-men. In all things, and toward all, we are enjoined to do as we would be done by. Nor should we forget that benevolent desires, after passing a certain point, can not undertake their own fulfillment without incurring the risk of evils beyond those sought to be remedied. Something may well be left to the graduated care of future legislation, and to heaven. In one point of view the coexistence of the two races in the South—whether the negro be bond or free—seems (even as it did to Abraham Lincoln) a grave evil. Emancipation has ridded the country of the reproach, but not wholly of the calamity. Especially in the present transition period for both races in the South, more or less of trouble may not unreasonably be anticipated; but let us not hereafter be too swift to charge the blame exclusively in any one quarter. With certain evils men must be more or less patient. Our institutions have a potent digestion, and may in time convert and assimilate to good all elements thrown in, however originally alien.

But, so far as immediate measures looking toward permanent Reestablishment are concerned, no consideration should tempt us to pervert the national victory into oppression for the vanquished. Should plausible promise of eventual good, or a deceptive or spurious sense of duty, lead us to essay this, count we must on serious consequences, not the least of which would be divisions among the Northern adherents of the Union. Assuredly, if any honest Catos there be who thus far have gone with us, no longer will they do so, but oppose us, and as resolutely as hitherto they have supported. But this path of thought leads toward those waters of bitterness from which one can only turn aside and be silent.

But supposing Re-establishment so far advanced that the Southern seats in Congress are occupied, and by men qualified in accordance with those cardinal principles of representative government which hitherto have prevailed in the land—what then? Why, the Congressmen elected by the people of the South will—represent the people of the South. This may seem a flat conclusion; but, in view of the last five years, may there not be latent significance in it? What will be the temper of those Southern members? and, confronted by them, what will be the mood of our own representatives? In private life true reconciliation seldom follows a violent quarrel; but, if subsequent intercourse be unavoidable, nice observances and mutual are indispensable to the prevention of a new rupture. Amity itself can only be maintained by reciprocal respect, and true friends are punctilious equals. On the floor of Congress North and South are to come together after a passionate duel, in which the South, though proving her valor, has been made to bite the dust. Upon differences in debate shall acrimonious recriminations be exchanged? shall censorious superiority assumed by one section provoke defiant self-assertion on the other? shall Manassas and Chickamauga be retorted for Chattanooga and Richmond? Under the supposition that the full Congress will be composed of gentlemen, all this is impossible. Yet, if otherwise, it needs no prophet of Israel to foretell the end. The maintenance of Congressional decency in the future will rest mainly with the North. Rightly will more forbearance be required from the North than the South, for the North is victor.

But some there are who may deem these latter thoughts inapplicable, and for this reason: Since the test-oath operatively excludes from Congress all who in any way participated in Secession, therefore none but Southerners wholly in harmony with the North are eligible to seats. This is true for the time being. But the oath is alterable; and in the wonted fluctuations of parties not improbably it will undergo alteration, assuming such a form, perhaps, as not to bar the admission into the National Legislature of men who represent the populations lately in revolt. Such a result would involve no violation of the principles of democratic government. Not readily can one perceive how the political existence of the millions of late Secessionists can permanently be ignored by this Republic. The years of the war tried our devotion to the Union; the time of peace may test the sincerity of our faith in democracy.

In no spirit of opposition, not by way of challenge, is any thing here thrown out. These thoughts are sincere ones; they seem natural—inevitable. Here and there they must have suggested themselves to many thoughtful patriots. And, if they be just thoughts, ere long they must have that weight with the public which already they have had with individuals.

For that heroic band—those children of the furnace who, in regions like Texas and Tennessee, maintained their fidelity through terrible trials—we of the North felt for them, and profoundly we honor them. Yet passionate sympathy, with resentments so close as to be almost domestic in their bitterness, would hardly in the present juncture tend to discreet legislation. Were the Unionists and Secessionists but as Guelphs and Ghibellines? If not, then far be it from a great nation now to act in the spirit that animated a triumphant town-faction in the Middle Ages. But crowding thoughts must at last be checked; and, in times like the present, one who desires to be impartially just in the expression of his views, moves as among sword-points presented on every side.

Let us pray that the terrible historic tragedy of our time may not have been enacted without instructing our whole beloved country through terror and pity; and may fulfillment verify in the end those expectations which kindle the bards of Progress and Humanity.

FROM *CLAREL*

Epilogue

If Luther's day expand to Darwin's year,
Shall that exclude the hope—foreclose the fear?

   Unmoved by all the claims our times avow,
The ancient Sphinx still keeps the porch of shade;
And comes Despair, whom not her calm may cow,
And coldly on that adamantine brow
Scrawls undeterred his bitter pasquinade.
But Faith (who from the scrawl indignant turns)
With blood warm oozing from her wounded trust,
Inscribes even on her shards of broken urns
The sign o' the cross—*the spirit above the dust!*

   Yea, ape and angel, strife and old debate—
The harps of heaven and dreary gongs of hell;
Science the feud can only aggravate—
No umpire she betwixt the chimes and knell:
The running battle of the star and clod
Shall run forever—if there be no God.

   Degrees we know, unknown in days before;
The light is greater, hence the shadow more;
And tantalized and apprehensive Man
Appealing—Wherefore ripen us to pain?
Seems there the spokesman of dumb Nature's train.
   But through such strange illusions have they passed
Who in life's pilgrimage have baffled striven—
Even death may prove unreal at the last,
And stoics be astounded into heaven.

Then keep thy heart, though yet but ill-resigned—
Clarel, thy heart, the issues there but mind;
That like the crocus budding through the snow—
That like a swimmer rising from the deep—
That like a burning secret which doth go
Even from the bosom that would hoard and keep;
Emerge thou mayst from the last whelming sea,
And prove that death but routs life into victory.

FROM *JOHN MARR AND OTHER STORIES*

John Marr

John Marr, toward the close of the last century born in America of a mother unknown, and from boyhood up to maturity a sailor under divers flags, disabled at last from further maritime life by a crippling wound received at close quarters with pirates of the Keys, eventually betakes himself for a livelihood to less active employment ashore. There, too, he transfers his rambling disposition acquired as a sea-farer.

After a variety of removals, at first as a sailmaker from sea-port to sea-port, then adventurously inland as a rough bench-carpenter, he, finally, in the last-named capacity, settles down about the year 1838 upon what was then a frontier-prairie, sparsely sprinkled with small oak-groves and yet fewer log-houses of a little colony but recently from one of our elder inland States. Here, putting a period to his rovings, he marries.

Ere long a fever, the bane of new settlements on teeming loam, and whose sallow livery was certain to show itself, after an interval, in the complexions of too many of these people, carries off his young wife and infant child. In one coffin, put together by his own hands, they are committed with meager rites to the earth—another mound, though a small one, in the wide prairie, nor far from where the mound-builders of a race only conjecturable had left their pottery and bones, one common clay, under a strange terrace serpentine in form.

With an honest stillness in his general mien — swarthy and black-browed, with eyes that could soften or flash, but never harden, yet disclosing at times a melancholy depth — this kinless man had affections which, once placed, not readily could be dislodged or resigned to a substituted object. Being now arrived at middle-life, he resolves never to quit the soil that holds the only beings ever connected with him by love in the family tie. His log-house he lets to a new-comer, one glad enough to get it, and dwells with the household.

While the acuter sense of his bereavement becomes mollified by time, the void at heart abides. Fain, if possible, would he fill that void by cultivating social relations yet nearer than before with a people whose lot he purposes sharing to the end — relations superadded to that mere work-a-day bond arising from participation in the same outward hardships, making reciprocal helpfulness a matter of course. But here, and nobody to blame, he is obstructed.

More familiarly to consort, men of a practical turn must sympathetically converse, and upon topics of real life. But, whether as to persons or events, one cannot always be talking about the present, much less speculating about the future; one must needs recur to the past, which, with the mass of men, where the past is in any personal way a common inheritance, supplies to most practical natures the basis of sympathetic communion.

But the past of John Marr was not the past of these pioneers. Their hands had rested on the plow-tail, his upon the ship's helm. They knew but their own kind and their own usages; to him had been revealed something of the checkered globe. So limited unavoidably was the mental reach, and by consequence the range of sympathy, in this particular band of domestic emigrants, hereditary tillers of the soil, that the ocean, but a hearsay to their fathers, had now through yet deeper inland removal become to themselves little more than a rumor traditional and vague.

They were a staid people; staid through habituation to monotonous hardship; ascetics by necessity not less than through moral bias; nearly all of them sincerely, however narrowly, religious. They were kindly at need, after their fashion; but to a man wonted—as John Marr in his previous homeless sojournings could not but have been—to the free-and-easy tavern-clubs affording cheap recreation of an evening in certain old and comfortable sea-port towns of that time, and yet more familiar with the companionship afloat of the sailors of the same period, something was lacking. That something was geniality, the flower of life springing from some sense of joy in it, more or less. This their lot could not give to these hard-working endurers of the dispiriting malaria,— men to whom a holiday never came,—and they had too much of up-rightness and no art at all or desire to affect what they did not really feel. At a corn-husking, their least grave of gatherings, did the lone-hearted mariner seek to divert his own thoughts from sadness, and in some degree interest theirs, by adverting to aught removed from the crosses and trials of their personal surroundings, naturally enough he would slide into some marine story or picture, but would soon recoil upon himself and be silent, finding no encouragement to proceed. Upon one such occasion an elderly man—a blacksmith, and at Sunday gatherings an earnest exhorter—honestly said to him, "Friend, we know nothing of that here."

Such unresponsiveness in one's fellow-creatures set apart from facti-tious life, and by their vocation—in those days little helped by machinery —standing, as it were, next of kin to Nature; this, to John Marr, seemed of a piece with the apathy of Nature herself as envisaged to him here on a prairie where none but the perished mound-builders had as yet left a durable mark.

The remnant of Indians thereabout—all but exterminated in their re-cent and final war with regular white troops, a war waged by the Red Men for their native soil and natural rights—had been coerced into the occupancy of wilds not very far beyond the Mississippi—wilds *then*, but now the seats of municipalities and States. Prior to that, the bisons, once streaming countless in processional herds, or browsing as in an endless battle-line over these vast aboriginal pastures, had retreated, dwindled in number, before the hunters, in main a race distinct from the agricultural pioneers, though generally their advance-guard. Such a double exodus of man and beast left the plain a desert, green or blossoming indeed, but almost as forsaken as the Siberian Obi. Save the prairie-hen, sometimes startled from its lurking-place in the rank grass; and, in their migratory season, pigeons, high overhead on the wing, in dense multitudes eclipsing the day like a passing storm-cloud; save these—there being no wide woods with their underwood—birds were strangely few.

Blank stillness would for hours reign unbroken on this prairie. "It is the bed of a dried-up sea," said the companionless sailor—no geologist— to himself, musing at twilight upon the fixed undulations of that immense alluvial expanse bounded only by the horizon, and missing there the stir that, to alert eyes and ears, animates at all times the apparent solitudes of the deep.

But a scene quite at variance with one's antecedents may yet prove suggestive of them. Hooped round by a level rim, the prairie was to John Marr a reminder of ocean.

With some of his former shipmates, *chums* on certain cruises, he had contrived, prior to this last and more remote removal, to keep up a little correspondence at odd intervals. But from tidings of anybody or any sort he, in common with the other settlers, was now cut off; quite cut off, except from such news as might be conveyed over the grassy billows by the last-arrived prairie-schooner—the vernacular term, in those parts and times, for the emigrant-wagon arched high over with sailcloth and voyaging across the vast champaign. There was no reachable post-office as yet; not even the rude little receptive box with lid and leather hinges, set up at convenient intervals on a stout stake along some solitary green way, affording a perch for birds, and which, later in the unintermitting advance of the frontier, would perhaps decay into a mossy monument, attesting yet another successive overleaped limit of civilized life; a life which in America can to-day hardly be said to have any western bound but the ocean that washes Asia. Throughout these plains, now in places overpopulous with towns overopulent; sweeping plains, elsewhere fenced off in every direction into flourishing farms—pale townsmen and hale farmers alike, in part, the descendants of the first sallow settlers; a region that half a century ago produced little for the sustenance of man, but to-day launching its superabundant wheat-harvest on the world; — of this prairie, now everywhere intersected with wire and rail, hardly can it be said that at the period here written of there was so much as a traceable road. To the long-distance traveler the oak-groves, wide apart, and varying in compass and form; these, with recent settlements, yet more widely separate, offered some landmarks; but otherwise he steered by the sun. In early midsummer, even going but from one log-encampment to the next, a journey it might be of hours or good part of a day, travel was much like navigation. In some more enriched depressions between the long, green, graduated swells, smooth as those of ocean becalmed receiving and subduing to its own tranquillity the voluminous surge raised by some far-off hurricane of days previous, here one would catch the first indication of advancing strangers either in the distance, as a far sail at sea, by the glistening white canvas of the wagon, the wagon itself wading through the rank vegetation and hidden by it, or, failing that, when near to, in the ears of the team, peaking, if not above the tall tiger-lilies, yet above the yet taller grass.

Luxuriant, this wilderness; but, to its denizen, a friend left behind anywhere in the world seemed not alone absent to sight, but an absentee from existence.

Though John Marr's shipmates could not all have departed life, yet as subjects of meditation they were like phantoms of the dead. As the growing sense of his environment threw him more and more upon retrospective musings, these phantoms, next to those of his wife and child, became spiritual companions, losing something of their first indistinctness and putting on at last a dim semblance of mute life; and they were lit by that aureola circling over any object of the affections in the past for reunion with which an imaginative heart passionately yearns.

◆ ◆ ◆ ◆ ◆

He invokes these visionary ones, — striving, as it were, to get into verbal

communion with them, or, under yet stronger illusion, reproaching
them for their silence: —

Since as in night's deck-watch ye show,
Why, lads, so silent here to me,
Your watchmate of times long ago?

Once, for all the darkling sea,
You your voices raised how clearly,
Striking in when tempest sung;
Hoisting up the storm-sail cheerly,
Life is storm — let storm! you rung.
Taking things as fated merely,
Child-like though the world ye spanned;
Nor holding unto life too dearly,
Ye who held your lives in hand —
Skimmers, who on oceans four
Petrels were, and larks ashore.

O, not from memory lightly flung,
Forgot, like strains no more availing,
The heart to music haughtier strung;
Nay, frequent near me, never staleing,
Whose good feeling kept ye young.
Like tides that enter creek or stream,
Ye come, ye visit me, or seem
Swimming out from seas of faces,
Alien myriads memory traces,
To enfold me in a dream!

I yearn as ye. But rafts that strain,
Parted, shall they lock again?
Twined we were, entwined, then riven,
Ever to new embracements driven,

Shifting gulf-weed of the main!
And how if one here shift no more,
Lodged by the flinging surge ashore?

Nor less, as now, in eve's decline,
Your shadowy fellowship is mine.
Ye float around me, form and feature:—
Tattooings, ear-rings, love-locks curled;
Barbarians of man's simpler nature,
Unworldly servers of the world.
Yea, present all, and dear to me,
Though shades, or scouring China's sea.

Whither, whither, merchant-sailors,
Whitherward now in roaring gales?
Competing still, ye huntsman-whalers,
In leviathan's wake what boat prevails?
And man-of-war's men, whereaway?
If now no dinned drum beat to quarters
On the wilds of midnight waters—
Foemen looming through the spray;
Do yet your gangway lanterns, streaming,
Vainly strive to pierce below,
When, tilted from the slant plank gleaming,
A brother you see to darkness go?

But, gunmates lashed in shotted canvas,
If where long watch-below ye keep,
Never the shrill *"All hands up hammocks!"*
Breaks the spell that charms your sleep,
And summoning trumps might vainly call,
And booming guns implore—
A beat, a heart-beat musters all,
One heart-beat at heart-core.

It musters. But to clasp, retain;
  To see you at the halyards main—
  To hear your chorus once again!

Tom Deadlight

During a tempest encountered homeward-bound from the Mediterranean, a grizzled petty-officer, one of the two captains of the forecastle, dying at night in his hammock, swung in the *sick-bay* under the tiered gun-decks of the British *Dreadnaught*, 98, wandering in his mind, though with glimpses of sanity, and starting up at whiles, sings by snatches his good-bye and last injunctions to two messmates, his watchers, one of whom fans the fevered tar with the flap of his old sou'-wester. Some names and phrases, with here and there a line, or part of one; these, in his aberration, wrested into incoherency from their original connection and import, he involuntarily derives, as he does the measure, from a famous old sea-ditty, whose cadences, long rife, and now humming in the collapsing brain, attune the last flutterings of distempered thought.

Farewell and adieu to you noble hearties,—
  Farewell and adieu to you ladies of Spain,
For I've received orders for to sail for the Deadman,
  But hope with the grand fleet to see you again.

I have hove my ship to, with main-top-sail aback, boys;
  I have hove my ship to, for to strike soundings clear—
The black scud a' flying; but, by God's blessing, dam' me,
  Right up the Channel for the Deadman I'll steer.

I have worried through the waters that are called the Doldrums,
  And growled at Sargasso that clogs while ye grope—
Blast my eyes, but the light-ship is hid by the mist, lads:—
  Flying Dutchman—odds bobbs—off the Cape of Good Hope!

But what's this I feel that is fanning my cheek, Matt?
    The white goney's wing? — how she rolls! — 't is the Cape! —
Give my kit to the mess, Jock, for kin none is mine, none;
    And tell *Holy Joe* to avast with the crape.

Dead reckoning, says *Joe*, it won't do to go by;
    But they doused all the glims, Matt, in sky t' other night.
Dead reckoning is good for to sail for the Deadman;
    And Tom Deadlight he thinks it may reckon near right.

The signal! — it streams for the grand fleet to anchor.
    The captains — the trumpets — the hullabaloo!
Stand by for blue-blazes, and mind your shank-painters,
    For the Lord High Admiral, he's squinting at you!

But give me my *tot*, Matt, before I roll over;
    Jock, let's have your flipper, it's good for to feel;
And don't sew me up without *baccy* in mouth, boys,
    And don't blubber like lubbers when I turn up my keel.

Jack Roy

Kept up by relays of generations young
Never dies at halyards the blithe chorus sung;
While in sands, sounds, and seas where the storm-petrels cry,
Dropped mute around the globe, these halyard singers lie.
Short-lived the clippers for racing-cups that run,
And speeds in life's career many a lavish mother's-son.

But thou, manly king o' the old *Splendid*'s crew,
The ribbons o' thy hat still a-fluttering, should fly —
A challenge, and forever, nor the bravery should rue.
Only in a tussle for the starry flag high,

When 't is piety to do, and privilege to die,
Then, only then, would heaven think to lop
Such a cedar as the captain o' the *Splendid*'s main-top:
A belted sea-gentleman; a gallant, off-hand
Mercutio indifferent in life's gay command.
Magnanimous in humor; when the splintering shot fell,
"Tooth-picks a-plenty, lads; thank 'em with a shell!"

Sang Larry o' the Cannakin, smuggler o' the wine,
At mess between guns, lad in jovial recline:
"In Limbo our Jack he would chirrup up a cheer,
The martinet there find a chaffing mutineer;
From a thousand fathoms down under hatches o' your Hades,
He'd ascend in love-ditty, kissing fingers to your ladies!"

Never relishing the knave, though allowing for the menial,
Nor overmuch the king, Jack, nor prodigally genial.
Ashore on liberty, he flashed in escapade,
Vaulting over life in its levelness of grade,
Like the dolphin off Africa in rainbow a-sweeping—
Arch iridescent shot from seas languid sleeping.

Larking with thy life, if a joy but a toy,
Heroic in thy levity wert thou, Jack Roy.

The Man-of-War Hawk

Yon black man-of-war hawk that wheels in the light
O'er the black ship's white sky-s'l, sunned cloud to the sight,
Have we low-flyers wings to ascend to his height?

No arrow can reach him; nor thought can attain
To the placid supreme in the sweep of his reign.

Old Counsel

OF THE YOUNG MASTER OF A WRECKED
CALIFORNIA CLIPPER

Come out of the Golden Gate,
Go round the Horn with streamers,
Carry royals early and late;
But, brother, be not over-elate—
All hands save ship! has startled dreamers.

The Tuft of Kelp

All dripping in tangles green,
Cast up by a lonely sea,
If purer for that, O Weed,
Bitterer, too, are ye?

The Maldive Shark

About the Shark, phlegmatical one,
Pale sot of the Maldive sea,
The sleek little pilot-fish, azure and slim,
How alert in attendance be.
From his saw-pit of mouth, from his charnel of maw
They have nothing of harm to dread,
But liquidly glide on his ghastly flank
Or before his Gorgonian head;
Or lurk in the port of serrated teeth
In white triple tiers of glittering gates,
And there find a haven when peril's abroad,
An asylum in jaws of the Fates!

They are friends; and friendly they guide him to prey,
Yet never partake of the treat—
Eyes and brains to the dotard lethargic and dull,
Pale ravener of horrible meat.

The Berg

A DREAM

I saw a ship of martial build
(Her standards set, her brave apparel on)
Directed as by madness mere
Against a stolid iceberg steer,
Nor budge it, though the infatuate ship went down.
The impact made huge ice-cubes fall
Sullen, in tons that crashed the deck;
But that one avalanche was all—
No other movement save the foundering wreck.

Along the spurs of ridges pale,
Not any slenderest shaft and frail,
A prism over glass-green gorges lone,
Toppled; nor lace of traceries fine,
Nor pendant drops in grot or mine
Were jarred, when the stunned ship went down.

Nor sole the gulls in cloud that wheeled
Circling one snow-flanked peak afar,
But nearer fowl the floes that skimmed
And crystal beaches, felt no jar.
No thrill transmitted stirred the lock
Of jack-straw needle-ice at base;

Towers undermined by waves—the block
Atilt impending—kept their place.
Seals, dozing sleek on sliddery ledges
Slipt never, when by loftier edges
Through very inertia overthrown,
The impetuous ship in bafflement went down.

Hard Berg (methought), so cold, so vast,
With mortal damps self-overcast;
Exhaling still thy dankish breath—
Adrift dissolving, bound for death;
Though lumpish thou, a lumbering one—
A lumbering lubbard loitering slow,
Impingers rue thee and go down,
Sounding thy precipice below,
Nor stir the slimy slug that sprawls
Along thy dead indifference of walls.

from *Pebbles*

V

Implacable I, the old implacable Sea:
    Implacable most when most I smile serene—
Pleased, not appeased, by myriad wrecks in me.

VII

Healed of my hurt, I laud the inhuman Sea—
Yea, bless the Angels Four that there convene;
For healed I am even by their pitiless breath
Distilled in wholesome dew named rosmarine.

FROM *TIMOLEON*

The Ravaged Villa

In shards the sylvan vases lie,
    Their links of dance undone,
And brambles wither by thy brim,
    Choked fountain of the sun!
The spider in the laurel spins,
    The weed exiles the flower:
And, flung to kiln, Apollo's bust
    Makes lime for Mammon's tower.

Monody

To have known him, to have loved him
    After loneness long;
And then to be estranged in life,
    And neither in the wrong;
And now for death to set his seal—
    Ease me, a little ease, my song!

By wintry hills his hermit-mound
    The sheeted snow-drifts drape,
And houseless there the snow-bird flits
    Beneath the fir-trees' crape:
Glazed now with ice the cloistral vine
    That hid the shyest grape.

In a Church of Padua

In vaulted place where shadows flit,
An upright sombre box you see:

A door, but fast, and lattice none,
But punctured holes minutely small
In lateral silver panel square
Above a kneeling-board without,
Suggest an aim if not declare.

Who bendeth here the tremulous knee
No glimpse may get of him within,
And he immured may hardly see
The soul confessing there the sin;
Nor yields the low-sieved voice a tone
Whereby the murmurer may be known.

Dread diving-bell! In thee inurned
What hollows the priest must sound,
Descending into consciences
    Where more is hid than found.

from *The Parthenon*

I: SEEN ALOFT FROM AFAR

Estranged in site,
Aerial gleaming, warmly white,
You look a suncloud motionless
In noon of day divine;
Your beauty charmed enhancement takes
In Art's long after-shine.

FROM *UNCOLLECTED POEMS*

Immolated

Children of my happier prime,
When One yet lived with me, and threw
Her rainbow over life and time,
Even Hope, my bride, and mother to you!
O, nurtured in sweet pastoral air,
And fed on flowers and light, and dew
Of morning meadows—spare, Ah, spare
Reproach; spare, and upbraid me not
That, yielding scarce to reckless mood
But jealous of your future lot,
I sealed you in a fate subdued.
Have I not saved you from the drear
Theft and ignoring which need be
The triumph of the insincere
Unanimous Mediocrity?
Rest therefore, free from all despite,
Snugged in the arms of comfortable night.

Pontoosuce

Crowning a bluff where gleams the lake below,
Some pillared pines in well-spaced order stand
And like an open temple show,
And here in best of seasons bland,
Autumnal noon-tide, I look out
From dusk arcades on sunshine all about.

Beyond the Lake, in upland cheer
Fields, pastoral fields, and barns appear,

They skirt the hills where lonely roads
Revealed in links thro' tiers of woods
Wind up to indistinct abodes
And faery-peopled neighborhoods;
While further fainter mountains keep
Hazed in romance impenetrably deep.

Look, corn in stacks, on many a farm,
And orchards ripe in languorous charm,
As dreamy Nature, feeling sure
Of all her genial labor done,
And the last mellow fruitage won,
Would idle out her term mature;
Reposing like a thing reclined
In kinship with man's meditative mind.

For me, within the brown arcade—
Rich life, methought; sweet here in shade
And pleasant abroad in air!—But, nay,
A counter thought intrusive played,
A thought as old as thought itself,
And who shall lay it on the shelf!—
I felt the beauty bless the day
In opulence of autumn's dower;
But evanescence will not stay!
A year ago was such an hour,
As this, which but foreruns the blast
Shall sweep these live leaves to the dead leaves past.

All dies!—
              I stood in revery long.
Then, to forget death's ancient wrong,
I turned me in the brown arcade,
And there by chance in lateral glade

I saw low tawny mounds in lines
Relics of trunks of stately pines
Ranked erst in colonnades where, lo!
Erect succeeding pillars show!

All dies! and not alone
The aspiring trees and men and grass;
The poet's forms of beauty pass,
And noblest deeds they are undone,
Even truth itself decays, and lo,
From truth's sad ashes fraud and falsehood grow.

All dies!
The workman dies, and after him, the work;
Like to these pines whose graves I trace,
Statue and statuary fall upon their face:
In very amaranths the worm doth lurk,
Even stars, Chaldæans say, have left their place.
Andes and Apalachee tell
Of havoc ere our Adam fell,
And present Nature as a moss doth show
On the ruins of the Nature of the æons of long ago.

But look—and hark!
                    Adown the glade,
Where light and shadow sport at will,
Who cometh vocal, and arrayed
As in the first pale tints of morn—
So pure, rose-clear, and fresh and chill!
Some ground-pine sprigs her brow adorn,
The earthy rootlets tangled clinging.
Over tufts of moss which dead things made,
Under vital twigs which danced or swayed,
Along she floats, and lightly singing:

"Dies, all dies!
The grass it dies, but in vernal rain
Up it springs and it lives again;
Over and over, again and again
It lives, it dies and it lives again.
Who sighs that all dies?
Summer and winter, and pleasure and pain
And everything everywhere in God's reign,
They end, and anon they begin again:
Wane and wax, wax and wane:
Over and over and over amain
End, ever end, and begin again—
End, ever end, and forever and ever begin again!"

She ceased, and nearer slid, and hung
In dewy guise; then softlier sung:
"Since light and shade are equal set
And all revolves, nor more ye know;
Ah, why should tears the pale cheek fret
For aught that waneth here below.
Let go, let go!"

With that, her warm lips thrilled me through,
She kissed me, while her chaplet cold
Its rootlets brushed against my brow
With all their humid clinging mould.
She vanished, leaving fragrant breath
And warmth and chill of wedded life and death.

Jonah's Song

The ribs and terrors in the whale,
    Arched over me a dismal gloom,

While all God's sun-lit waves rolled by,
    And lift me deepening down to doom.

I saw the opening maw of hell,
    With endless pains and sorrows there;
Which none but they that feel can tell—
    Oh, I was plunging to despair.

In black distress, I called my God,
    When I could scarce believe him mine,
He bowed his ear to my complaints—
    No more the whale did me confine.

With speed he flew to my relief,
    As on a radiant dolphin borne;
Awful, yet bright, as lightning shone
    The face of my Deliverer God.

My song for ever shall record
    That terrible, that joyful hour;
I give the glory to my God,
    His all the mercy and the power.

From Moby-Dick

Billy in the Darbies

Good of the Chaplain to enter Lone Bay
And down on his marrow-bones here and pray
For the likes just o' me, Billy Budd.—But, look:
Through the port comes the moon-shine astray!
It tips the guard's cutlass and silvers this nook;
But 'twill die in the dawning of Billy's last day.

A jewel-block they'll make of me tomorrow,
Pendant pearl from the yard-arm-end
Like the ear-drop I gave to Bristol Molly—
O, 'tis me, not the sentence they'll suspend.
Ay, Ay, all is up; and I must up too
Early in the morning, aloft from alow.
On an empty stomach, now, never it would do.
They'll give me a nibble—bit o' biscuit ere I go.
Sure, a messmate will reach me the last parting cup;
But, turning heads away from the hoist and the belay,
Heaven knows who will have the running of me up!
No pipe to those halyards.—But aren't it all sham?
A blur's in my eyes; it is dreaming that I am.
A hatchet to my hawser? All adrift to go?
The drum roll to grog, and Billy never know?
But Donald he has promised to stand by the plank;
So I'll shake a friendly hand ere I sink.
But—no! It is dead then I'll be, come to think.—
I remember Taff the Welshman when he sank.
And his cheek it was like the budding pink.
But me they'll lash me in hammock, drop me deep
Fathoms down, fathoms down, how I'll dream fast asleep.
I feel it stealing now. Sentry, are you there?
Just ease these darbies at the wrist,
And roll me over fair,
I am sleepy, and the oozy weeds about me twist.

From Billy Budd

About the Editor

Robert Penn Warren was born April 24, 1905, in Guthrie, Kentucky. After graduating summa cum laude *from Vanderbilt University (1925), he received a master's degree from the University of California (1927), did graduate work at Yale University (1927–28) and then at Oxford as a Rhodes Scholar (B.Litt., 1930). Mr. Warren has published many books and has been the recipient of numerous awards and honors. In 1944 Mr. Warren occupied the Chair of Poetry of the Library of Congress. A novel,* All the King's Men *(1946), was awarded the Pulitzer Prize for fiction.* Promises *(1957) won the Pulitzer Prize for poetry, the Edna St. Vincent Millay Prize of the Poetry Society of America and the National Book Award. In 1959 he was elected to the American Academy of Arts and Letters. He received the Bollinger Prize in Poetry for* Selected Poems: New and Old 1923–1966 *in 1967. His collection* Now and Then: Poems 1976–1978 *won the Pulitzer Prize for Poetry in 1979. In 1986 Mr. Warren was appointed Poet Laureate of the United States. His most recent book is* A Place To Come To *(1986). He lives in Connecticut with his wife, Eleanor Clark.*